WATCHMAN NEE

# SEPARATION FROM THE WORLD

*Living Stream Ministry*
Anaheim, California

3

First Edition, November 1997.

ISBN 1-57593-959-2

Published by

*Living Stream Ministry*
2431 W. La Palma Ave., Anaheim, CA 92801 U.S.A.
P. O. Box 2121, Anaheim, CA 92814 U.S.A.

*Printed in the United States of America*

02　03　04　05　/　10　9　8　7　6　5　4　3

# SEPARATION FROM THE WORLD

Scripture Reading: Exo. 10:8-11, 21-26; 12:6-11, 37-42; 2 Cor. 6:17

There are many commandments in the Bible concerning separation from the world. The Old Testament contains many examples and teachings concerning this. For example, Egypt, Ur of the Chaldees, Babylon, and Sodom are all types of the world. They show different aspects of the world. Egypt represents the joy of the world, Ur of the Chaldees represents the religions of the world, the tower of Babel represents the confusion of the world, and Sodom represents the sins of the world. A man should come out of Egypt and also out of Ur of the Chaldees, just as Abraham did. Lot went to Sodom, and the people of Israel fell into captivity in Babylon. All should come out from these places. The Bible uses four different places to represent the world and shows how God's people come out from these different aspects of the world.

## I. THE TYPE OF ISRAEL'S EXODUS FROM EGYPT

## A. The Result of Redemption Being to Go Out

God saved the Israelites through the Passover lamb. When the messenger of God went forth to kill the firstborn in the land of Egypt, the angel of death passed over the doors which had the blood upon them. If there was no blood on the door, the firstborn of that house was killed. It had nothing to do with whether the door was good or bad, whether there was anything special about the lintel or the side posts, whether there was anything good about that family, or whether the firstborn child honored his parents. The issue was whether there was any blood. Whether or not you will perish does not depend on your family's status or your behavior; it depends on whether you have the blood. The basic factor for salvation is the blood; this has nothing to do with us.

We who are saved by grace are redeemed by the blood. But please remember that immediately after being redeemed by the blood, we must move and go out. Do not think that we can buy a house and dwell in Egypt after we are redeemed by the blood. Those who are redeemed by the blood must set out that very night. The lamb was slaughtered before midnight, and the blood was sprinkled with hyssop. They ate their meal quickly, with their loins girded and their staff in their hands, because they had to leave immediately.

The first result of redemption is separation, that is, departure, a going out. God never redeems a person and leaves him in the old position to continue living in the world. There is absolutely no such thing. Once a person is born again, saved, he must take up his staff and set out. Once the angel of destruction has done his work of separating the saved from the perishing, the saved ones must leave. Once you have been separated by the smiting angel, you have to pack up and move out of Egypt.

A staff is for walking. No one holds a staff to lie down in bed. The staff is not a pillow; it is for walking. All those who are redeemed, old or young, must take their staff and leave the same night. As soon as you are redeemed by the blood, you become a sojourner and a pilgrim on the earth; you have to go out of Egypt and be separated from the world immediately. You must not continue to live there.

There was a sister who taught a class in a children's meeting. Once she was telling the story of Lazarus and the rich man. She asked the children, "Do you want to be Lazarus or the rich man? The rich man enjoys himself in this age and suffers in the next. Lazarus suffers today and enjoys himself later. Which would you choose to be?" An eight-year-old girl stood up and said, "While I am alive, I want to be the rich man, but when I die, I want to be Lazarus." Many people are like this. When they need salvation, they trust in the blood of the Lamb; but after they are saved by the blood, they settle down firmly in Egypt. They think that they can have the best of both sides.

Please remember that the blood's redemption saves you from the world. Once you are redeemed by the blood, you immediately become a sojourner, a pilgrim in this world. This does not mean that you no longer live on the earth. It means that you are immediately separated from the world. Wherever redemption is applied, this is the result. As soon as a man is redeemed, his course is changed, and he has to leave the world. The separation of the blood separates the living from the dead; it also separates the children of God from the people of the world. Once we are redeemed, we can no longer remain in the world.

### B. The Many Frustrations from Pharaoh

The story of Israel's exodus from Egypt shows us how difficult it was for them to leave Egypt! Egypt tried to hold them back again and again. When the Israelites first wanted to leave Egypt, Pharaoh only allowed the strong men to go; the young and the old had to stay back. Pharaoh knew that if he could hold back the young and the old the strong men would not go far. After a while they would come back. Satan's strategy is to prevent us from having a thorough separation from Egypt. From the very beginning, Moses rejected Pharaoh's delays. If we leave one thing or one person behind, we cannot go too far; eventually we will turn back.

You may recall what Pharaoh told Moses the first time: "Go ye, sacrifice to your God in the land" (Exo. 8:25). Later, he told him not to go too far. The third time he told him that only the strong ones could go. The fourth time, he told him that all the people could go but the cattle and the sheep had to remain. Pharaoh's way was to persuade them to serve God there in Egypt. This was his basic premise. He was willing to allow a person to be God's child as long as such a one remained in Egypt. He knew that if a person served God in Egypt, he would not have a testimony and he would have to serve Pharaoh in the end. Even though one wanted to be God's servant, he would eventually end up being Satan's servant.

If you try to serve God in the world, you will surely end up being Satan's slave. You will have to make bricks for him, and he will not let you go. Even if he does, he will not let you go too far. If he lets you go, he may only allow the strong men to go; the rest will have to stay. Satan is quite familiar with the words in Matthew 6:21: "For where your treasure is, there will your heart be also." The treasure and the person go together. He knew that if Pharaoh held back the cattle and the sheep, the people would not go too far. The people eventually would follow the cattle and the sheep. But God wanted the cattle and the sheep to follow the people. He wanted the people to be saved from the treasure.

After a person is saved, he must go out to the wilderness. Moreover, he has to bring all the people and all his treasures with him. Otherwise, he will eventually go back to Egypt, and there will be no separation from Egypt. God's commandment is that those who serve Him must separate themselves from the world.

### C. Our Way Being in the Wilderness

Just to confess the Lord with our mouth and say, "I have believed in the Lord today," is not enough for a testimony. We must come out from the world and be separated. This takes us one step further than confessing Jesus as Lord with our mouth. We cannot be dumb Christians. However, opening up our mouth alone is not enough; we must be separated from the world. We cannot continue our previous friendships, social ties, or other previous relationships. We must treasure our present position in the Lord and turn far away from our previous position. The person has to go out, and the possessions have to go out as well. Others may say that we are foolish, but we should not listen to them. Today we have to come out from Egypt. From the time we become a Christian, our way is that of the wilderness, not of Egypt.

In New Testament terms, both Egypt and the wilderness represent the world. Egypt refers to the world in its moral sense. The wilderness refers to the world in its physical sense. Christians are in the physical world but not in the moral world. We must see that there are two aspects of the world: the first as a place and the second as a system. There are many things related to the physical world which are attractive, which arouse the lusts of the eyes, the lusts of the flesh, and the vainglory of life. This is Egypt. But there is another meaning to the world—the physical world as a place where one's body resides.

## D. Leaving the Moral World

Today we Christians must come out of the system and the organization of the world. Leaving the world refers to our deliverance from the moral world, not the physical world. We need to leave the moral world behind, not the physical world. In other words, we are still living in the world, but this world has become a wilderness to us.

What is the world to us? Mr. D. M. Panton put it well when he said, "While I am living, it is a journey to me; when I die, it is a tomb to me." While a believer is living on this earth, the world is a journey to him; when he dies, the world is only a tomb in which he is buried. We must be separated from the people of the world. Every believer must be separated from the world. In the eyes of the world, we are in the wilderness; we are pilgrims. They are the ones who are in the world.

## E. Sojourners and Pilgrims in this World

We must realize that we are sojourners and pilgrims in this world. As far as the moral world is concerned, we have come out of it. It wants to keep us, but if we stay, we will not be able to serve God. The world wants to be closer to us, but if we allow it to come too close to us, it will be impossible for us to serve God. The world wants to keep our people and our treasure, but if these things are kept in the world, we will not be able to serve our God.

We have been separated from Egypt, and our faces are toward the promised land. The basis of that separation is the blood, the blood that has bought us back. The Egyptians have not been bought by the blood; the worldly ones have not been redeemed. As redeemed ones, we have been transferred to another world. Therefore, we must leave this world.

Suppose you go to a watch shop to buy a watch. What do you do after you have bought it? Once the purchase has been made, you take the watch away. I should not buy the watch and leave it behind. I should not tell the proprietor, "Here, you use it!" This is not reasonable. Buying means taking away. Whenever there is a purchase, there is a taking away. If I buy a sack of rice, the rice is taken away from the shop. After one buys something, the purchased item is taken away. Please remember that since the blood has bought us, we must be taken away from the world. Once a person is bought by the Lord's blood, he should leave for the promised land. As soon as one is bought, he should leave. Those who are not bought can stay behind. But as soon as a person is bought, he should leave. Once a person is bought, he has no choice but to go with the Lord. If I have been bought by the Lord, I must leave the world and go with Him.

## II. AREAS THAT REQUIRE SEPARATION
## FROM THE WORLD

You may ask what we should separate ourselves from. What things are considered the world? What areas should we be separated from? Before we touch any specific item, we should realize that our heart and spirit are the first things that need separation from the world. If a person's heart is set towards the world, it becomes futile to speak to him about anything else. It is useless to try to be delivered from a hundred things if the person himself still remains in the world. First, there must be a deliverance of the person, a deliverance of the spirit, and a deliverance of the heart. Deliverance from matters comes later.

A man must be separated completely from Egypt; he must be separated from the world. He should not be afraid that others will criticize him as being peculiar. Then there is the need to take care of some principles. In some areas we should be separated from the world, while in other areas we should maintain peace with it. We have no intention to be contentious. In the family, in the office, and everywhere, we do not want to arouse controversy. Let us consider five specific things that need to be dealt with:

### A. Things Which the World Considers
### Improper for Christians to Do

We should refrain from anything that the world considers

improper for Christians to do. Our Christian life at the minimum should meet the standard of the worldly people. Everyone in the world has set up a yardstick and a standard for Christians. If you do not meet this standard, you have failed them. When you do something, you should not give the Gentiles any ground to ask, "Do Christians do this?" If others say this, you are finished. As soon as you are rebuked, you are finished. Suppose you are caught visiting certain places. The Gentiles may say, "Do Christians come to places such as this?" There are many places Gentiles like to visit. If you tell them that it is wrong to visit those places, they may insist and argue with you. But if you visit those places yourself, they will ask, "How can you also go to these places?" Some matters are sinful. When the Gentiles do them, they keep quiet about it. But if you do the same things, they will speak up. Therefore, we must refrain from things that the Gentiles consider improper. This is a minimum requirement. When a Gentile says, "Christians should not do such a thing," we should turn away from it immediately.

Some young people are saved, but their parents are still unsaved. Sometimes these children ask for something from the parents. The parents may say, "Do you Christians want these things as well?" It is most shameful for a Christian to find himself adjusted by the Gentiles. Abraham lied and was rebuked by Abimelech. This is a most shameful thing in the Bible. We must refrain from things that are considered improper by the Gentiles. We must stay away from things that the worldly people, the Egyptians, consider inappropriate for Christians to do. We must be separated from them.

## B. Things Incompatible with the Lord

Anything that is incompatible with the Lord must also be removed. Since the Lord suffered humiliation on the earth, we should not seek glory here. Since the Lord was crucified like a robber, we should not seek to be welcomed everywhere. When our Lord was walking on the earth, He was accused of demon possession. We cannot allow people to say that we have the best mind, that we are smart, or that we are very intellectual. We have to pass through what the Lord passed through. Everything that is incompatible with the Lord must go.

The Lord said that a slave is not greater than his master and a disciple is not greater than his teacher. If the world treated our Master one way, we should not expect it to treat us another way. If it treated our Teacher one way, we should not expect it to treat us another way. If we are not treated the same as our Master, something is wrong with us, and something is definitely wrong in our relationship with the Lord. Whatever our Lord experienced on the earth should be our experience today.

To follow Jesus of Nazareth, one must be ready to suffer humiliation; this is not a thing of glory. To follow Jesus of Nazareth means to bear the cross. When others first came to the Lord, the Lord told them that they had to bear the cross in order to follow Him. According to the Lord, this is the main entrance. He does not wait until a person is in the room before He tells him this condition. Before we go in, the Lord makes it clear that we must bear the cross in order to follow Him. The Lord has called us to bear the cross. This is the way we are taking, and we can only follow the Lord according to this way. The Lord's relationship with the world should be our relationship with the world. Our relationship with the world must be compatible with our Lord's relationship with the world; we cannot take a different way.

Galatians 6:14 shows us that the cross stands between the world and the Lord. The Lord is on one side, and the world is on the other side. The cross stands in between. We and the world stand on opposite sides of the cross. The world crucified our Lord on the cross; therefore, the world is on the other side of the cross. Since I am on the Lord's side, I would have to go through the cross before I could reach the world. There is no way to go around the cross because the cross is a fact; it is also history. I cannot annul this fact, and I cannot annul history. The world has crucified our Lord. I cannot take another way. If the cross is a fact, the crucifixion of the world to me is also an eternal fact. If I cannot annul the cross, I also cannot annul the fact that the world has been crucified to me. Today there is no way for me to go to the world's side, unless I remove the cross. The cross is here, and I have no way to avoid it because the crucifixion of my Lord is a fact. Today, I am a person on the other side of the cross.

Suppose a person's parents or brothers are killed. Others may offer a reasonable excuse for the murderer, but the person may say, "My folks are already dead. An excuse cannot change this fact. If my folks were not yet dead, there would be something to talk about. But now that they are dead, there is nothing more to say." In the same principle, we can say that the cross is already here; what more is there to say? The world has already crucified our Lord on the cross. Today, we are on the Lord's side, and we can only say, "World, from your point of view, I am crucified. From my point of view, you are also crucified." Today, it is impossible for these two sides to communicate. It is impossible for the world to come over. It is also impossible for us to go over. The cross is a fact. If I have no way to annul the cross, I have no way to win the world over to my side. My Lord has died, and there is no longer any possibility of reconciliation.

Once we see the cross we can say, "I boast in the cross." As far as we are concerned, the world is crucified on the cross. As far as the world is concerned, we are crucified on the cross (Gal. 6:14). The cross will be forever history and a fact. As Christians, we are on one side, while the world is on the other side. The cross is in between. As soon as we open our eyes, we will see nothing but the cross. If we want to see the world, we have to see the cross first.

A new believer must be led by the Lord to see that his condition should match the Lord's condition. Some people ask many questions. They ask, "Will we touch the world if we do this?" And they ask, "Can we do that?" We cannot tell people what to do item by item. We only need to give them the general principle. The world is against the cross; it is against our Lord. If our heart is open and soft before God and if we go to Him, the difference between the world and the cross spontaneously will become clear to us.

As soon as we go to the Lord, we will find out what the world is and what the world is not. We only need to ask,

"What is my relationship with this matter, and what was the Lord Jesus' relationship with it while He was on the earth?" As long as our relationship with the world is the same as the Lord's, we are all right. If our position is different from the Lord's position, we have erred. The Lamb was slain, and we are the followers of the Lamb. We are those who follow the Lamb wherever He may go (Rev. 14:4). We take the same stand as that of the Lord. Anything that is not on the same ground as the Lord or that stands against the Lord is the world, and we must depart from it.

## C. Anything That Quenches
## Our Spiritual Life

It is difficult for us to point out the world item by item; the list is endless. But we should grasp one basic principle: everything that quenches one's spiritual life in the Lord is the world. The world is anything that kills one's zeal for prayer to God. The world is anything that takes away one's interest in God's Word. The world is anything that frustrates one from testifying before men. The world is anything that hinders one from coming to the Lord, anything that results in confession. The world is an atmosphere that chokes and dries a person up. It is anything that discourages a man's heart from loving and yearning for the Lord. Here we see a broad princi- ple—anything that quenches our spiritual condition before the Lord is the world. We must reject all of it.

Some people say, "This thing is not sinful at all. Can you say that it is worldly?" Many things appear to be very good to our eyes, but they quench the fire within us after we touch them once or twice. Our conscience becomes weak before God. After we become involved with these things, our Bible reading becomes tasteless. We may have the time, but we no longer have the heart for reading. After we participate in such things, we feel empty inside and have nothing to testify before men. Such things may not be a matter of sin. Our question is whether or not these things are quenching our spiritual life. Everything that quenches our spiritual life is the world and must be rejected totally before the Lord.

### D. Everything That Fails to Give Others the Impression That We Are Christians

We need to mention one more thing—our relationship with other people. Any kind of social function, communication, or activity that causes us to hide our lamp under the bushel is the world. Many social friendships, functions, and contacts with worldly people force us to put our lamp under the bushel; there is no way under those circumstances for us to stand up to declare that we are Christians. When others engage in such conversation, you have to pretend to be courteous. You have to listen to them and laugh with them. You feel quenched within, but you have to put on a smiling face. Inwardly you feel that this is the world, yet outwardly you have to go along with it. Inwardly you know this is sin, yet outwardly you cannot say that it is wrong. You should not remain in this kind of social environment. Many of God's children are gradually sucked into the world through indiscriminate social activities and contacts.

All new believers must know where they stand from the very beginning, and they must make a choice. We are not trying purposely to be antisocial. We are not John the Baptist who did not eat or drink. We follow our Lord who ate and drank. But when we contact people, we must maintain our stand. No one should be able to insult our Christian stand. They should respect our stand. When I take a stand as a Christian, I must maintain my stand even if others criticize me.

If we really want to take the way of separation from the world, we must pay attention to our speaking. We must also show our Christian stand every time we are in the company of others. If we cannot maintain our stand as Christians, it is better to turn away from where we are. Psalm 1:1 says that we should not "stand on the path of sinners, / Nor sit in the company of mockers." If we stand on the path of sinners, we will end up in their place sooner or later. If we sit in the company of mockers, we will become mockers sooner or later. Sin and mocking are contagious. We must learn to flee these things as if we are fleeing from germs.

## E. Things Disapproved of by Weak Believers

Things which stumble a weak conscience are another class of things that constitute the world. God's children must learn to turn away from them. The previous discussion concerns things which the world considers improper. Here we are talking about things which a young Christian considers improper. If a Gentile thinks that we should not do a certain thing, we will lose our testimony if we do it. Similarly, we should avoid anything that a Christian disapproves of, even if the one who disapproves is the youngest and weakest of all Christians. This is the biblical commandment. It is not the words of the strong Christian but the words of the weak Christian that should determine what we should or should not do. What they say may not be correct; what they consider forbidden may not be wrong. But we should not stumble them because their conscience is weak. They may think that we are on the wrong way. If we take such a way, we will stumble them. Paul said, "All things are lawful to me, but not all things are profitable" (1 Cor. 6:12). All things are lawful, but others may consider these things to be a form of the world. Therefore, we should not do them for their sake.

Paul spoke of the example of eating meat. He said that if eating meat would stumble a brother, he would never eat meat. This is not easy. Who can abstain from meat forever? Paul's word does not suggest that one should not eat meat. In 1 Timothy he clearly said that it is wrong to abstain from meat. However, he showed us that he was willing to carry such caution to the extreme. It did not matter to him whether or not he ate meat. He might have been clear about what he was doing, but others who followed him may not have known what he was doing. We may know at which point we should stop, but those who follow may not know this. What would happen if they take a few steps further? There is nothing wrong if we eat meat, but after awhile those who follow us may go to the temple to eat the sacrifices or perhaps worship the idols as well. Many things may not be directly related to the world, but we should still exercise care in touching them because others may consider them a form of the world.

### III. COMING OUT FROM THEIR MIDST
### TO BE WELCOMED BY THE ALL-SUFFICIENT LORD

Second Corinthians 6:17-18 says, "Therefore 'come out from their midst and be separated, says the Lord, and do not touch what is unclean; and I will welcome you'; 'and I will be a Father to you, and you will be sons and daughters to Me, says the Lord Almighty.'"

In the New Testament the words Lord Almighty are used for the first time in 2 Corinthians 6. *Lord Almighty* is *Elshadai* in Hebrew. *El* is God, *sha* is a mother's breast or milk, and *shadai* means something that is with milk. In Hebrew *shadai* means "all-sufficient." The words *Almighty God* in the Old Testament are also *Elshadai,* which should be translated as "the All-sufficient God." The mother's milk is all that a child needs. The mother's breasts contain the milk; all the supply is in the breasts. The root of the word *shadai* is "the mother's breast." This means that with God we have everything.

Second Corinthians 6:17 tells us that if we come out from their midst and do not touch their unclean things, God will welcome us and be a Father to us. We shall be sons and daughters to Him, says the *All-sufficient* Lord. We can see that these words have not been spoken lightly. The Lord is saying, "Because of Me you have left many things. You have come out from their midst and are separated from them. You have terminated your relationships with them and are no longer touching their unclean things. Your two hands are empty, and there is nothing left in you. Now that you have done all this, I will welcome you."

Please remember that everyone who feels welcomed by the Lord is separated from the world. Many people do not feel the excellency of the Lord when they come to Him because they have not counted all things as refuse. Those who have not counted all things as refuse surely consider earthly things precious. Such people do not know what it means for God to welcome them; they do not know what it means for God to be their Father and for them to be God's children. They do not know that the One who spoke these words is the all-sufficient Lord. Can you see the special significance of the word *shadai?* The words *Lord Almighty* are used here because when a person has cast away everything, he needs God as the *Shadai;* he needs a Father who is all-sufficient.

Psalm 27:10 tells us that if our father and mother forsake us, Jehovah will take us up. In other words, He becomes our father. Psalm 73:26 says that when our flesh and our heart fail, God is the rock of our heart and our portion forever. Herein lies the sweetness of our experience. There must be loss on one side before there can be gain on the other side. The blind man met the Lord only after he was cast out of the synagogue (John 9:35). If we remain in the synagogue, we will never meet the Lord. But when we are cast out, we see the Lord's blessing upon us immediately.

As new believers we must come out from the world. Only then will we taste the Lord's sweetness. Once we drop something on one side, we will taste the goodness of the Lord on the other side.